A BASKET OF
BERRIES

Then seek your job with thankfulness and work till further orders,
If it's only netting strawberries or killing slugs on borders;
And when your back stops aching and your hands begin to harden,
You will find yourself a partner in the Glory of the Garden.

Rudyard Kipling, *The Glory of the Garden*

A BASKET OF
BERRIES

Recipes and paintings from
a fruit garden

VAL ARCHER

HARMONY BOOKS   NEW YORK

Published by Harmony Books, a division of Crown
Publishers, Inc., 201 East 50th Street, New York, New
York 10022.
Member of the Crown Publishing Group.
Random House, Inc., New York, Toronto, London,
Sydney, Auckland

Originally published in Great Britain in 1993 by
Pavilion Books Limited.

HARMONY and colophon are trademarks of
Crown Publishers, Inc.

Manufactured in Italy

Library of Congress Cataloging-in-Publication Data is
available from the publisher.

ISBN 0-517-59274-6

1 3 5 7 9 10 8 6 4 2

First American Edition

CONTENTS

INTRODUCTION

At home we had three gardens. The first was my father's allotment where he grew all our vegetables, very much a man's world of creosoted sheds perched on regimented plots lined by neatly cut grass paths and tended with a dig-for-victory fervour by an army of men who arrived on bikes. They grew potatoes in deep trenches, Brussels sprouts and cabbages, runner beans elegantly twining around slim avenues of canes, squat onions and bronze shallots for pickling, parsnips, turnips, carrots and a tangle of peas (usually Kelvedon Wonder) on a hedge of dead twigs. Even horseradish for the Sunday roast beef had its place, but flowers and fruit were banned; there seemed to be wordless acknowledgement that they were too frivolous a crop for the serious business of feeding the nation.

The front garden was all for show, a velvet lawn (no children allowed), roses, peonies and a rockery. Aubretia lined the path and clarissa hedges separated us from next door.

The back garden felt as if it were all mine, a friendly lawn pitted and scruffy from numerous attempts to erect tents made of wooden clothes-horses and old curtains, sweet-smelling lavender bushes, four apple trees to climb, a dozen brown hens and the fruit garden. In a small space my parents had managed to plant enough fruit bushes to supply all our needs and to have plenty more to give away in presents of jams and jellies to anyone who called in. There were raspberry canes and loganberries, redcurrant and blackcurrant bushes draped with black nets, two sorts of gooseberry and a rather unsuccessful strawberry patch nestling on straw next to the rhubarb, which forced its way through the broken bottom of an upturned galvanized bucket. Every autumn we went blackberry picking to the nearby woods, armed with walking sticks to pull down the highest brambles, and two baskets, one for the berries, the other to hold dead twigs gathered for kindling the winter fires.

Summer for me started with my first breakfast of redcurrants, picked by my mother, sprinkled with sugar and served jewel-bright in a favourite blue bowl. Our kitchen from then on seemed to be full of berries: bottled in Kilner jars, bubbling in saucepans on the stove, in batches of jam waiting to be labelled and dripping through muslin jelly bags into white china bowls, the whole house filled with their rich perfume and brilliant colour. There were of course the endless tasks of topping and tailing gooseberries and blackcurrants, picking over raspberries and blackberries and strigging tassels of redcurrants with a fork, but the rewards were great: berry pies for dinner, fresh jams and scones for tea, and every salad had a sprinkling of currants or raspberries. While my mother cooked, I had my place at the other end of the kitchen table, my watercolours laid out in small round pans glowing like fruit sweets. I was eight years old when I painted my first berry picture and have loved growing, painting, cooking and eating them ever since.

The purpose of this book is, in a small way, to communicate this love and, I hope, to encourage you to grow and cook with berries. Berries are not difficult to grow, and many varieties are ideally suited to small gardens; growing strawberries in hanging baskets, for example, is a great success, and

fraises des bois thrive on a sunny windowsill. The pleasures of tending the plants, waiting for the flowers to be pollinated and watching the fruits swell and turn from green through yellow to red, black or blue repay a thousand times the little extra work involved in reorganizing your garden and enriching its soil conditions.

The botanical definition of a berry is that it contains one or more seeds enclosed within a single structure. The seeds do not have any stony hard coat around them and are contained in a soft pulpy flesh formed from the ovary wall. So, botanically, a cucumber is a berry and a strawberry is not. For the purposes of this book I have chosen fruit which has the popular rather than the botanical status as berry and within that category have selected the ones that give me most pleasure by virtue of their colour, shape, texture, taste and, I must admit, nostalgic association.

GOOSEBERRIES

How the gooseberry acquired its name is the subject of much debate, but it is probably because the fruit was served with goose when it became widely cultivated in England in the early sixteenth century. (Many children give it an even more frivolous name: goosegog.)

Since Tudor times, gooseberry crumbles, fools, jellies, sauces and pies have featured on English tables. To this day competitors in the shows organized by eight Gooseberry Clubs in Cheshire in the north of England compete for the Premier Berry with fruits the size of hen's eggs.

Gooseberries favour cool, damp climates and thus thrive in northern latitudes. A single plant will produce 6lbs to 12lbs of fruit – left untended a bush will continue to produce fruit for many years. However, winter and summer pruning, spraying against mildew and protection against birds in many areas are necessary to ensure an abundant crop.

Sweet white, yellow and red gooseberries are dessert fruits and are usually served fresh: let them lie in hot sunshine until warm before serving – it brings out the sweetness and flavour. For sweet and savoury sauces, fools and other creamed desserts, as fillings for pies, puddings and tarts, and for jellies, chutneys and jams choose the smaller and harder green gooseberry.

Savoury gooseberry sauce is traditionally served with fried or grilled mackerel. It also enhances other fish dishes, cold roast pork, roast goose and rich meat dishes such as ossi buchi, where the tomatoes in the traditional recipe can be replaced with gooseberries. Sweet gooseberry sauce is delicious hot or cold, with stewed puddings, ice creams and fruit flans.

BORDAGE
LE FIEF SAUVIN
49600 BEAUPREAU
Poids net:100g

MACKEREL BAKED IN A PARCEL

2 whole medium mackerel (bluefish),
about 300–350g/10–12oz, gutted and
cleaned with heads and tails on
sunflower or safflower oil
salt and freshly ground black pepper
a few whole gooseberries, topped and tailed
a few sprigs fresh fennel

Preheat the oven to 190°C/375°F/Gas 5.
Cut the baking parchment or kitchen foil
into an oval shape large enough to make a
loose tent to completely enclose the fish
without touching it. With a brush, lightly oil
each piece of paper or foil. Season the cavity
of each fish and stuff with a
few whole gooseberries and
a frond or two of fennel,

Serves 2

and insert gooseberries and fennel fronds into
three diagonal cuts made in the skin. Lay the
fish on the paper or foil and carefully draw
together and fold the paper over the fish or
scrunch together the edges of the foil. The
parcels should be airtight, so no juices or
steam can escape during cooking.

Place the parcels on a baking tray and bake
in the preheated oven for about 20–25
minutes, or until the fish are just cooked.

GOOSEBERRY SAUCE

For centuries this was a popular sauce in France for serving with a whole baked mackerel, hence the popular French name for green gooseberries – *groseilles à maquereau*, 'mackerel berries'. They add a pleasant sharpness to this sauce, which acts as a good foil for the rich, oily flesh of fish such as mackerel or bluefish.

450g/1lb gooseberries, topped
and tailed
30g/1oz/2tbsp butter
salt and freshly ground white pepper
sugar
freshly grated nutmeg

Put the gooseberries and 2 tbsp water in a small saucepan, cover and simmer over low heat for about 15–20 minutes or until the fruit is tender.

Pass the fruit through a sieve or liquidize in a blender. Return the purée to a clean pan and add the butter. Season to taste with salt and pepper and add just enough sugar to take the edge off the fruit (the sauce should not be sweet). Simmer gently, uncovered, for about 2 minutes. Just before serving season lightly with freshly grated nutmeg.

Serves 2

GOOSEBERRY FOOL

450g/1lb gooseberries
1 head of sweetly scented elderflowers
120g/4oz/½ cup caster (superfine) sugar
500ml/16fl oz/2 cups thick (heavy)
cream for whipping

Gently cook the gooseberries with the
elderflowers, sugar and 2tbsp water in a small
covered saucepan for 10–15 minutes until
they turn yellow and soft. Remove from the
heat, discard the elderflowers, and mash the
berries down gently, adding more sugar if
you wish. Allow to cool.

Meanwhile, whip the cream in a bowl until
soft peaks form – do not overwhip. Fold the
gooseberries into the cream, and chill.

Serve with Nut Shortbread.

Serves 6

NUT SHORTBREAD

120g/4oz/¾ cup hazelnuts or
filberts, shelled
300g/10oz/2½ cups plain (all-purpose) flour
2tsp baking powder
pinch of salt
120g/4oz/½ cup caster (superfine)
sugar, plus extra for dredging
60g/2oz/⅓ cup ground rice
250g/8oz/1 cup butter, softened

Preheat the oven to 150°C/300°F/Gas 2
Grease four flat baking sheets.

Roast the nuts on a baking tray in the
oven for about 5 minutes or until just
coloured. Allow to cool slightly and
rub off the skins. Roughly chop the
nuts. Put the flour, baking powder, salt,
sugar and ground rice into a basin and
rub in the butter. Add the chopped nuts and
knead together well. Divide the mixture into
four rounds. Roll the mixture out into four
circles approximately 1cm/½in thick. Crimp
the edges, mark each shortbread into six with
a sharp knife, and lightly prick all over with a
knitting needle or fork.

Bake for 45 minutes to an hour until lightly
coloured. Check the shortbread after 20
minutes, and turn the oven down to
130°C/250°F/Gas ½, if necessary. Remove
from the oven and dredge lightly with sugar.
Mark into slices with a sharp knife and cool
on a wire rack.

Makes 24 pieces

STRAWBERRIES

As early as 200 BC strawberries were cultivated by the Romans. In the sixteenth century they were sold in cone-shaped straw baskets and thus became one of the earliest packaged foods. Strawberries are not difficult to grow and there is a variety to suit most gardens. They give a quicker return than any other fruit; plants set out in late summer will provide a crop the following June. For small gardens, they can be grown in tubs and growing bags and are ideally suited, both practically and visually, to hanging baskets and window boxes.

Eat strawberries as soon as possible after they are picked. Look for bright, firm and unblemished fruit with a fresh, green calyx. Try to avoid washing strawberries as they absorb water easily, which makes them soft and flavourless. If you have to rinse them do so before hulling, but it is usually enough to brush them clean. Strawberries are at their most enjoyable when they are served plain, with vanilla sugar and cream, or sprinkled with a teaspoon of balsamic vinegar. With strawberries and cream serve a Sauterne or a similarly sweet Bordeaux or Vouvray Moelleux. Try a strawberry soup, use them for sorbets and ice creams, for shortcake, to adorn tarts and piled high on a sponge base. Freshly made waffles with strawberry sauce are a real treat as are the awful sounding but tasty strawberry fritters.

COLD POACHED SALMON

Court bouillon is made by simmering for 10 minutes half a bottle of dry
white wine, three times that quantity of water, celery, carrots,
an onion, parsley, a bay leaf, thyme, salt and a few peppercorns. Strain before use.

*1 whole salmon, weighing about
1.4kg/3lb, dressed with head and
tail on
about 1.5 litres/2½ pints/1½ quarts
court bouillon (see above)
juice of 1 lemon
salt and freshly ground black pepper
lemon wedges and mixed green salad
leaves, to serve*

Place the fish in a large saucepan or fish kettle
and cover completely with the court
bouillon. Add the lemon juice, and season.
Bring the liquid gently to the boil over a
medium heat, then cover the pan, reduce the
heat and poach very gently (the water should
just tremble) for 1 minute. Turn off the heat
and allow the fish to cool in the stock for at
least four hours.

Arrange the fish on a serving platter
surrounded by the salad leaves. Decorate
with lemon wedges and serve with home-
made mayonnaise.

Serves 4–6

SALAD ELONA

This refreshing summer salad makes an excellent accompaniment for a fine fish such as poached salmon, although it also goes well with cold chicken. Make it just before serving.

1 medium cucumber, peeled
16 large strawberries, hulled
salt
caster (superfine) sugar
freshly ground black pepper
2tbsp white wine vinegar or
strawberry vinegar (see p.75)

Cut the cucumber and the strawberries into thin slices. Arrange in concentric circles on a plate, alternating rings of cucumber with rounds of strawberries.

Season with a pinch each of salt and sugar, plenty of freshly ground black pepper, and drizzle evenly with the vinegar.

Serves 4–6

STRAWBERRY TARTLETS

FOR THE PASTRY
*220g/7oz/scant 2 cups plain (all-
purpose) flour
45g/1½oz/3tbsp caster (superfine) sugar
large pinch baking powder
90g/3oz/6tbsp chilled butter, cut into dice
1 egg, beaten with ½tsp vanilla extract*

FOR THE FILLING
*150g/5oz/⅔ cup fromage frais
orange-flower water
honey
450g/1lb strawberries, hulled*

To make the pastry, sift together the flour, sugar and baking powder. Rub the butter into this mixture until it resembles fine

breadcrumbs. Add the egg and vanilla and knead rapidly into a ball. Wrap in greaseproof (waxed) paper and chill for about an hour until firm.

Meanwhile, preheat the oven to 180°C/350°F/Gas 4, and lightly grease eight small individual tartlet tins.

Roll out the pastry to 3mm/⅛in thick and use to line the prepared tartlet tins. Cover with greaseproof (waxed) paper and weigh down with dried beans. Bake on the middle shelf of the oven for 5–6 minutes or just until the pastry has set.

Remove from the oven. Take off the paper and beans, prick the pastry lightly all over with a fork and bake for 8–10 minutes more until the tartlets begin to brown slightly. Remove the cases from the tins while still warm and allow to cool on a wire rack.

To make the filling, turn out the fromage frais into a small bowl and add orange-flower water and honey to taste. Reserve and chill. Just before serving, spoon the perfumed fromage frais into the cold tartlet shells and top with the strawberries.

Makes 8 tartlets

CHOCOLATE-DIPPED STRAWBERRIES

250g/8oz dark (bittersweet) chocolate,
broken into small pieces
60g/2oz/4tbsp butter
250–350g/8–12oz large, dry, firm
strawberries with leaves intact

Line a baking (cookie) sheet with lightly oiled greaseproof (waxed) paper.

Put the chocolate pieces in a bowl with the butter and place over a saucepan of simmering water over medium heat. Using a wooden spoon, stir occasionally for about 5 minutes until the chocolate has melted.

Reduce the heat to low and pick up a strawberry by its leaves. Dip two-thirds of the berry into the chocolate. Put it on the paper and leave to set. Repeat with the remaining berries and, if necessary, refrigerate until ready to serve.

Eat these soon after they are made, or the fruit softens and the juices begin to run.

STRAWBERRY JAM

1.6kg/3¹/₂lb hulled strawberries
1.4kg/3lb/6 cups preserving sugar
juice of ¹/₂ lemon

Choose strawberries that are small and have a good, strong flavour. Cut the larger berries in half. Put all the fruit in a non-metallic bowl and gently mix in the sugar. Cover with plastic film and allow to stand for 8 hours.

Pour the mixture into a large wide saucepan or preserving pan. Stir gently over low heat until all the sugar has dissolved, then increase the heat to high. Cook at a rolling boil for 15 minutes or just until setting point is reached, removing any scum that forms on the surface.

To test for setting point, remove the pan from the heat and spoon a small quantity of the jam on to a *cold* saucer from the refrigerator. Allow the jam to cool a little then draw your finger across the surface. It will wrinkle if it is ready. If it doesn't wrinkle, return the pan to the heat and bring

26

the mixture back to the boil. Continue to boil and repeat the test until setting point is reached. Be careful not to overcook the jam.

Stir the lemon juice into the mixture in the pan, remove any scum, and pour the jam into sterilized jars. Seal at once with discs of wax paper and cover when cold.

Makes 2.7kg/6lb

WILD STRAWBERRIES

The wild strawberry is a tiny, fragrant fruit that grows all over Europe and other temperate areas. Wild strawberries and their cultivated cousin the Alpine strawberry – *fraises des bois* – can be found growing in woods and scrub on rich soils and basic grassland. In Cornwall, in south-west England, they can occasionally be found growing on the wooded banks of country lanes.

Alpine strawberries can be grown in the smallest of spaces, and are well worth cultivating, as just a few will perfume a mixed fruit salad or tart. Sow the seeds in autumn, pricking out when the shoots are 6mm high, plant out in window boxes, hanging baskets or pots in early spring, water regularly and feed fortnightly. Baron Solemacher is the most popular variety of alpine strawberry. Unlike the truly wild strawberry it does not produce runners, prefers partial shade to full sun, and produces fruit continuously throughout the summer.

The best way to eat wild strawberries is the simplest way, as they are eaten in France: served with crème fraîche or covered in a good red Bordeaux wine, with the remainder of the bottle and a glass to the side.

WILD STRAWBERRIES WITH LIQUEUR

True *fraises des bois* are such a rare treat that they are best eaten unadulterated, with a
simple liqueur poured over at the last minute and perhaps a few sweet
biscuits as an accompaniment.

350g/12oz wild strawberries
2tbsp orange- or almond-flavoured liqueur, to taste
langue de chat *biscuits or amaretti*
almond-flavoured biscuits

About 2 hours before serving, pick over the
strawberries and remove any dirt or grit.
Pour the liqueur over them and refrigerate
until ready to serve.

Spoon out into attractive serving dishes or
glasses, and serve accompanied by the
biscuits, and perhaps more liqueur.

Serves 4

Black, red and white currants are delicious soft berries that thrive in cool, moist climates and in places with a good summer rainfall.

Blackcurrants are easy to grow and are long-lived. Their flavour is quite sharp while the red and white varieties tend towards sweetness. Red and white currants, though related to the black varieties, do not have the same growing habits and grow as bushes or as cordons. White currants are an albino strain of red, as stunning to look at as they are

BLACK, RED & WHITE CURRANTS

delicious to eat – but luckily for growers, they are not liked as much as redcurrants by hungry birds.

Red and blackcurrants make excellent jams and jellies. They don't need to be cooked for long, so they retain their flavour and colour, and they have good setting qualities.

Redcurrants can add colour and a piquant flavour to salads. They are good with sliced peaches or nectarines and in compôtes, pastries, jams and jellies. They are also an essential ingredient of Summer Pudding (see p.49) and Cumberland sauce, the traditional accompaniment for certain game and lamb dishes. Redcurrant jelly is the best glaze for fruit tarts as well as being the traditional accompaniment to lamb and turkey.

Crème de cassis is an alcoholic beverage made from blackcurrants that a former major of Dijon and World War Two Resistance hero, Canon Kir, popularized. He added white wine to a small amount of the deep purple liqueur to make a refreshing drink.

Long gone are the days when redcurrants straight from the bush were transported to market in large wicker panniers by early-

morning trains to ensure their freshness. Today, red and white currants are still best enjoyed fresh and left on the stalks and served as dessert fruits in all their glistening beauty.

Frosted or glazed white currants make a luxurious decoration for cakes and fruit salads and can be poached lightly in a syrup flavoured with a liqueur to make a sauce for ice cream.

GOAT'S CHEESE CROSTINI
WITH ROCKET AND CURRANT SALAD

6 handfuls of rocket leaves
6 discs of goat's cheese log, or 3
  crottins, *cut in half*
120g/4oz mixed red and
  white currants

FOR THE DRESSING
1tbsp balsamic vinegar
1tbsp extra virgin olive oil
salt and freshly
  ground black pepper

FOR THE CROSTINI
1 loaf French bread (baguette)
extra virgin olive oil
1 clove garlic, cut in half

Preheat the grill or broiler.

Wash the rocket and drain it thoroughly. Pick off and discard any long stalks.

Mix together the ingredients for the dressing in a small bowl or jug.

To make the crostini, cut the French bread into six slices about 2.5cm/1in thick and brush on both sides with olive oil. Grill the slices on both sides until golden then rub one side with the cut garlic. Place a disc of goat's cheese on each of the crostini and arrange them on a heatproof (broiler-safe) dish.

Gently toss the rocket leaves in the dressing and arrange on individual serving plates. Sprinkle over the red and white currants.

Quickly brown the goat's cheese on the crostini under a hot grill, making sure the crostini do not burn. Arrange in the centre of the salad plates and serve while still warm.

Serves 6

GRILLED RED MULLET

This is a very easy dish to prepare and a highly attractive one too, for the vivid reds of the mullet and the currants in the herb butter are visually quite striking. The liver of the fish is much prized, but it is up to you whether to remove it or not before cooking.

Redcurrant and thyme butter,
to serve
6 red mullet (goat fish), weighing
250g/8oz each, dressed, with heads
and tails on
salt and freshly ground black pepper
60g/2oz/4tbsp unsalted
butter, melted
6 sprigs of fresh thyme, to garnish

Serves 6

First, prepare the redcurrant and thyme butter, then cut into six rounds, ready for serving. Preheat the grill or broiler.

Put the fish on the grilling tray and season well. Baste the fish with the melted butter and cook under the hot grill for about 8–10 minutes, turning once, and basting again during cooking.

Arrange the fish on a serving platter and top each one with redcurrant and thyme butter. Serve garnished with thyme.

REDCURRANT AND THYME BUTTER

120g/4oz redcurrants
1tbsp fresh chopped thyme or ¼tsp
dried thyme
2tbsp fresh lemon juice
sea salt and freshly ground black
pepper
120g/4oz/½ cup butter, softened

To garnish 6-8 fish

Put the redcurrants, thyme and lemon juice
in a small, heavy-bottomed saucepan and cook
over low heat for about 1–2 minutes or until
half of the berries have popped and released
their juices. Remove from the heat and set
aside to cool. Season with salt and pepper.

When the redcurrant mixture is completely
cold, beat it into the softened butter.
Refrigerate for about half an hour then wrap
in greaseproof paper and form into a log.
Return to the refrigerator to cool once more.
Cut into medium discs (about 15g/½oz in
weight) and serve with grilled fish or meat.

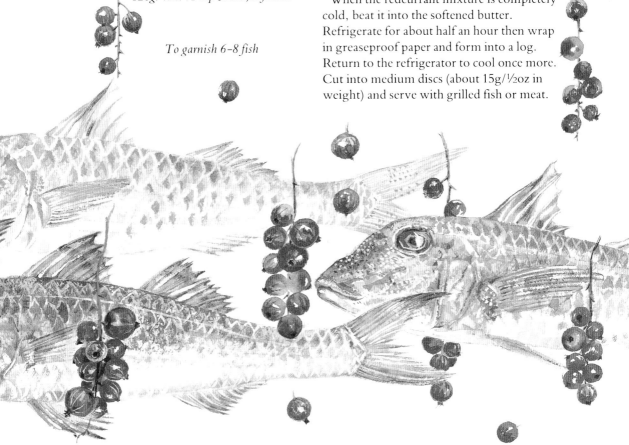

REDCURRANT OR
BLACKCURRANT JELLY

Clarity, colour and intense flavour are the distinctive features of these jellies.
Preserves made like this keep all the flavour of the fresh fruit and can
be used with cooked meat, on bread, or as a glaze for fruit tarts.

900g/2lb red or blackcurrants
preserving sugar

Remove the stalks from the blackcurrants –
there's no need to remove them from the
redcurrants – and rinse the fruit well in a large
sieve. Place in a preserving pan and heat
gently over medium heat until the juices
begin to run. Simmer the fruit gently,
uncovered, stirring occasionally with a
wooden spoon, for about 30 minutes until
softened. Pour into a jelly bag (or a strainer
lined with a damp clean cloth) set over a large

clean bowl. Allow the juice to drip through undisturbed for 4–6 hours, preferably overnight.

Measure the juice back into the preserving pan and set over medium heat. Calculate the amount of sugar required, allowing 450g/1lb/2 cups sugar to 500ml/16fl oz/2 cups juice.

Warm the sugar gently in a separate pan (do not allow it to colour), and add it to the juice, stirring constantly. Once all the sugar has completely dissolved, raise the heat to high and bring to the boil. Allow to boil hard for 1 minute, skim very quickly to remove any scum and pour at once into sterilized jars. Seal with discs of wax paper and cover when cool.

Makes 900g–1.4kg/2–3lb jelly

DUCK BREASTS WITH SAUCE CASSIS

This is an adaptation of Michel Guérard's way of cooking duck breasts without extra fat, which leaves them succulent and tasty.

2 duck breasts weighing about 350g/12oz

FOR THE SAUCE
250g/8oz blackcurrants, washed and de-stalked
150ml/5fl oz/²⁄₃ cup dry white wine
150ml/5fl oz/²⁄₃ cup meat stock
caster (superfine) sugar
90ml/3fl oz/6tbsp white wine vinegar or blackcurrant vinegar (see p.75)
2tbsp crème de cassis
30g/1oz/2tbsp butter
juice of a lemon
salt and freshly ground black pepper

To prepare the sauce, cook the fruit in a small saucepan with the wine, stock and 1 tbsp sugar for 10–15 minutes or until soft. Pour into a blender or food processor and blend until smooth. Pour the sauce into a saucepan and set aside.

In a small pan boil together the vinegar and 2 tsp sugar for about 5 minutes, until the liquid darkens and turns syrupy. Add this and the *crème de cassis* to the sauce. Keep warm while you cook the duck.

Heat a heavy casserole or iron broiler pan over medium heat and put the breasts in, skin-side down (no need to add fat). Cook them for 10 minutes if you like them pink, a little longer if you prefer them medium to well done. Turn them over and cook for a further 3–5 minutes. Remove them with a slotted spoon and keep warm while you finish the sauce.

Reheat the sauce gently and whisk in the butter; do not boil. Taste the sauce and correct the seasoning with a little lemon juice, salt and black pepper. To serve, spoon out the sauce on to four heated serving plates. Slice the breasts and fan out half of each in the pools of sauce. Serve at once.

Serves 4

CASSIS SORBET

450g/1lb blackcurrants, de-stalked
175g/6oz/¾ cup caster (superfine) sugar
2tsp lemon juice
crème de cassis, *to serve*

Cook the blackcurrants in a covered saucepan over medium heat with 90ml/3fl oz/6tbsp water for about 10 minutes or until the juices run freely and the currants have softened. Remove the lid, raise the heat and cook, stirring constantly, until the mixture has reduced to a thick purée. Place in an electric blender and liquidize before passing the mixture through a sieve.

To make the syrup, dissolve the sugar in 300ml/10fl oz/1¼ cups water in a heavy saucepan over low heat. Stir well with a wooden spoon and bring to the boil. Boil well for 5–10 minutes until the mixture becomes syrupy. Allow to cool slightly, then add the lemon juice. Mix together the syrup with the blackcurrants and, if necessary, add water to make up to 700ml/1¼ pints/ 3 cups. Pour into a freezer container, cover and freeze at the lowest possible temperature until firm. Remove the mixture when it is frozen round the edges and beat hard, preferably in a blender or food processor, until smooth. Repeat twice at 45-minute intervals.

Serves 6

STRAWBERRY ICE CREAM

350g/12oz ripe strawberries, hulled
2tbsp fresh lemon juice
1tbsp fresh orange juice
275g/9oz/generous cup caster (superfine) sugar
3 egg whites
450ml/¾ pint/scant 2 cups
whipping cream, lightly whipped

Purée the strawberries in a blender and pass
them through a fine sieve into a bowl. Mix in
the fresh fruit juices.

Put the sugar in a small saucepan and add
125ml/4fl oz/½ cup water. Stir over low heat
until the sugar dissolves completely. Raise the
heat and bring to the boil. Boil rapidly for
about 5 minutes or until the mixture thickens
slightly and becomes syrupy. (If you are
using a jam thermometer, this will be at
about 110°C/230°F.) Remove from heat when
correct consistency is reached.

While the syrup is boiling, whisk
the egg whites until stiff, then
whisk the syrup into them in a
slow stream. Keep whisking
until the mixture is thick and
glossy.

Fold the puréed strawberries
into the lightly whipped cream
then fold this into the egg-white mixture.
Freeze until firm.

Makes 10–12 servings

RASPBERRIES

The raspberry has been enjoyed for centuries as a dessert fruit and as an ingredient in sweets, wine and jams. The early herbalists knew it as Raspis; the scientific name, *idaeus*, comes from Mount Ida in Turkey where the plant grows in profusion. Raspberries are today cultivated throughout the world and there are many late fruiting varieties making them available well into the autumn.

Sometimes black raspberries can be found, as can yellow or white varieties, superior in flavour to red say many gardeners. Mrs Beeton, writing in 1861, praised both red and white raspberries.

Raspberries should be picked when they are ripe but still firm, and ideally when the fruit is dry. Eat or freeze as soon as possible – small, slightly unripe fruit is best for freezing (and raspberries freeze well). Do not wash, as they will quickly become waterlogged and shapeless.

Enjoy raspberries on their own or with cream and a little sugar and a good red Bordeaux wine. Raspberries, strawberries and blueberries go well together, as do raspberries and peaches. Poached peaches are delicious with vanilla ice cream and Melba sauce, a raspberry sauce created for the opera singer Nellie Melba by Escoffier, when he was working at The Savoy Hotel in 1892.

Raspberries complement food of a different texture – serve with cream on a soft sponge cake, baked in warm raspberry muffins, piled up on crisp, sweet meringues or served in a hollowed-out half-melon.

The acidity of raspberries makes them suitable for savoury dishes such as lamb and duck, and for game sauces and marinades. Raspberry vinegar can be mixed with sparkling mineral water to make a refreshing drink.

RASPBERRY AND ROSE PETAL PANCAKES

These pretty pancakes are a charming grown-up dessert.
They are also fun to make with children, who are fascinated by the idea
of eating rose petals.

FOR THE PANCAKES
*120g/4oz/1/2 cup plain (all-
purpose) flour
pinch of salt
2 large eggs
250ml/8fl oz/1 cup milk
1tbsp butter, melted
unsalted butter and oil for frying*

FOR THE FILLING
*175g/6oz/3/4 cup Greek-style
strained yogurt
1tbsp icing (confectioner's) sugar, or
more to taste
1dsp rosewater
175g/6oz raspberries*

TO SERVE
*petals from 2 pink roses
120g/4oz raspberries
icing (confectioner's) sugar*

To make the pancake batter, sift the flour and salt into a bowl. In another bowl, beat together the eggs and milk, then add the cooled melted butter. Pour the mixture into the flour, beat until smooth, and leave to stand for at least 1 hour. (You can do this by hand or in a food processor.)

Using a little butter or oil to grease a crêpe pan or frying pan, cook twelve small pancakes. Keep them warm while you make the filling.

Combine the yogurt, icing sugar and rosewater in a small bowl, then gently fold in the raspberries.

Gently remove the petals from the roses and tear off and discard the bitter base from each one. Set aside.

Place heaped tablespoonfuls of the filling mixture in the centre of each pancake and gently roll them up. Place two pancakes on the centre of individual serving plates, top with a few extra raspberries, sprinkle with sugar and scatter rose petals over the top.

Serves 6

SUMMER PUDDING

900g/2lb mixed red and black fruit,
such as blackberries, raspberries,
redcurrants, blackcurrants
250g/8oz/1 cup caster (superfine) sugar
slices of slightly stale white bread, crusts removed
thick (heavy) cream or crème fraîche, to serve

Put the fruit and sugar into a bowl and leave overnight. Lightly grease a 1 litre/1¾ pint/1 quart ceramic bowl with butter. Cut a circular slice of bread to snugly fit the bottom of the bowl, then cut most of the remaining bread into wedges and use to line the sides. Press the pieces together well so that there are no gaps.

Over a low heat, bring the fruit and sugar to the boil then simmer gently for 2–3 minutes or just until the fruit softens. Allow to cool slightly. Pour half the fruit into the bread-lined bowl, then put in one slice of bread and the remaining fruit and juice, saving a little juice to serve. Make a lid for the pudding with one or two slices of bread. Cover with a plate just large enough to fit on top of the pudding and weigh it down with a couple of cans. Refrigerate for at least 10 hours.

To serve, loosen the pudding by running a knife carefully between it and the bowl. Place a serving dish on top of the bowl, invert the whole thing quickly, and carefully remove the bowl. If the bread is not soaked through, pour over the reserved juice. Serve immediately, cut into wedges and accompanied by cream.

Serves 6

COEURS Á LA CRÈME WITH FRESH RASPBERRY COULIS

Traditionally the heart-shaped moulds were made of wicker; now china ones are used. If you decide to use cream cheese, make sure it is unsalted.

250g/8oz/1 cup curd, cottage or cream cheese
300ml/10fl oz/1¼ cups double (heavy) cream
2tbsp caster (superfine) sugar
2 egg whites
150ml/5fl oz/²⁄₃ cup single (light)
cream, to serve
250g/8oz raspberries, to serve

FOR THE RASPBERRY COULIS
300g/10oz fresh raspberries
120g/4oz/¹⁄₂ cup caster
(superfine) sugar
2tbsp lemon juice

Press the cheese through a fine sieve into a mixing bowl and stir in first the double cream then the sugar. Beat until light and fluffy. In a small bowl, beat the egg whites just until stiff. Fold them carefully into the cheese mixture.

Line six moulds with fine damp muslin or cheesecloth. Spoon the cheese into the prepared moulds, tapping the sides gently to allow the mixture to settle. Fold the ends of the cloth over the moulds, place them on a cake rack and refrigerate overnight.

To make the coulis, liquidize the raspberries and sugar to a smooth purée. Add lemon juice to taste. Pass through a sieve into a small bowl. To serve, spoon a little of the raspberry coulis on to each serving plate. Discard any draining liquid and unmould the heart-shaped desserts on top of the sauce. Drizzle with cream and surround with the raspberries.

LOGANBERRIES, BOYSENBERRIES & TAYBERRIES

The loganberry is said to have resulted from
an accidental cross between a blackberry
and a raspberry that took place in 1881 in the
garden of Judge Logan of Santa Cruz,
California. This fine hybrid is a plant of only
moderate vigour and thus is suitable for small
gardens; the stems are not so thorny as those
of the blackberry.

The loganberry is larger and softer than
both the raspberry and the blackberry and has
a distinctive slightly acidic taste.

The tayberry is larger than a loganberry.
Plant this fruit if you want only one hybrid
berry in your garden – growth isn't rampant
but yields are good. Remember to look out

for thornless varieties, as picking them is easier, and the flavour is as good. The tayberry is a hybrid of the raspberry and blackberry but in scent and flavour it is like a ripe blackberry.

The boysenberry looks like a longer plump blackberry – although the flavour is more akin to a wild raspberry. This fruit is a good choice for growing in sandy soils and the plant is remarkably drought-resistant.

All of these berries are as good to eat fresh with sugar and cream as any berry, and can be added to other fruits in a salad. Use them as an unusual ingredient in pies and puddings, for making into jams, jellies, sorbets and ice creams. They freeze well, with or without sugar. Like blackberries, loganberries and boysenberries go well with game dishes.

Arguably, of all the hybrids, none has so far achieved the superb, distinctive flavour of the loganberry.

LOGANBERRY THORNLESS

LOGANBERRIES WITH AMARETTI CREAM

This is a very simple way of serving any berries that at their best need no cooking or complicated embellishments.

250ml/8fl oz/1 cup thick
(heavy) cream
1–2tbsp Amaretto or other almond
liqueur, or to taste
8 amaretti biscuits
90g/3oz/¼ cup flaked almonds, toasted
450g/1lb loganberries or tayberries

Whip the cream in a bowl until soft peaks form. Add the Amaretto to taste and crumble in the biscuits. Turn into a bowl and top with the toasted almonds.

Spoon the loganberries into individual serving glasses and pass the Amaretti Cream separately with extra amaretti biscuits.

Serves 4

TURKISH ORANGE CAKE WITH FRESH TAYBERRIES OR LOGANBERRIES

1 large orange
120g/4oz/1 cup ground almonds
120g/4oz/½ cup caster
(superfine) sugar
1tsp baking powder
3 drops almond extract
3 large eggs
60g/2oz/¼ cup pine kernels

TO SERVE
450g/1lb fresh tayberries or
loganberries
icing (confectioner's) sugar
2 oranges

Put one whole orange in a small saucepan, cover with water and simmer for 2 hours. Pour away the water and leave to cool.

Preheat the oven to 180°C/350°F/Gas 4. Grease a 23cm/9in shallow cake tin and line with greaseproof (waxed) paper.

Chop the cooked orange roughly, discard the pips and liquidize, including the skin.

Mix together the ground almonds, sugar, baking powder and almond extract in a bowl. Beat the eggs with a fork, beat in the liquidized orange, then pour into the bowl containing the other ingredients and mix well. Pour this mixture into the prepared tin and sprinkle the top with pine kernels. Bake in the middle of the oven for 35 minutes, or until a skewer comes out clean. Leave to cool slightly, then turn out on to a wire rack.

Just before serving, peel off the paper and sprinkle the top of the cake with a little icing sugar. Serve in wedges with slices of orange and fresh tayberries or loganberries.

Serves 4

BLUEBERRIES

The bushy plant that produces blueberries originated in North America but is related to the native British bilberry, whortleberry or blaeberry, which has smaller fruit. The lowbush berry grows wild on rocky, acid soils to a height of about a foot, and delights American berry-gatherers the way the blackberry inspires the British. The highbush blueberry, which yields larger berries, can be cultivated in most sunny gardens in containers where the right soil conditions, acid and well-drained, can be maintained. Blueberries are slightly blander than bilberries though both are small, smooth, perfectly round and a mysteriously blue-black with a powdery bloom. This is an aristocratic fruit and one of America's favourite berries. Traditional American recipes make a virtue of its luscious taste: blueberry muffins, pancakes, bread, pies and cakes. For blueberry cheesecake use fromage frais rather than regular full-fat soft cheese to make a lighter version.

It must be on charcoal they flatten their fruit,
I taste in them sometimes the flavour of soot.
And after all, really they're ebony-skinned:
The blue's but a mist from the breath of the wind,
A tarnish that goes at a touch of the hand.

Robert Frost

BLUEBERRY GRIDDLE CAKES

*250g/8oz/2 cups plain
(all-purpose) flour
2 eggs
¼tsp salt
½ tsp caster (superfine) sugar
250ml/8fl oz/1 cup milk
175–250g/6–8oz blueberries, plus a
few extra to garnish
cream or crème fraîche and sugar,
to serve*

To make the batter, put all the ingredients
except the blueberries, cream and sugar in a
blender or food processor and mix. Pour into
a large bowl and leave to stand for an hour.
Fold in the berries just before you start
to cook.

Heat the frying-pan (griddle) until very hot and grease it lightly. Pour three separate tablespoonfuls of the batter on to the surface of the pan and fry for 2–3 minutes, turning once. Repeat with the remaining batter, keeping the griddle cakes warm while you complete the batch.

Garnish with a few extra berries and serve with cream or crème fraîche and sugar.

Serves 6

BLUEBERRY SOUP

This chilled soup makes a refreshing start to a
light meal on a hot summer's day. It can also
be served for dessert.

1.25kg/2½lb fresh blueberries, plus
a few extra to garnish
4 whole cloves
5cm/2in piece of cinnamon stick
150ml/5fl oz/⅔ cup honey
juice of 1 lemon
3tbsp crème de cassis
1tbsp blueberry vinegar (see p.75)

TO GARNISH
plain yogurt
grated fresh orange zest (rind)

Wash the berries, and remove and discard any
stems, leaves or discoloured berries. Tie up
the whole spices in a piece of muslin.

Put the berries in a large pan over medium
heat with 1 litre/32fl oz/1 quart water and the
spices. Bring to the boil and stir in the honey.
Reduce the heat and simmer, partially
covered, for about 10–15 minutes or until the
berries are very soft.

Remove the pan from the heat, discard the
spice bag and allow the fruit to cool. Pass the

mixture through a sieve or purée it in a
blender. Add the lemon juice, *crème de cassis*
and blueberry vinegar. Cover and chill
overnight, or for at least 8 hours.

Serve in soup bowls or dessert dishes,
garnished with a few of the reserved berries.
Swirl in a little yogurt and sprinkle each dish
with some grated orange zest.

Serves 6

SMOKED CHICKEN SALAD WITH BLUEBERRIES

1 large whole smoked chicken or
700–900g/1½–2lb smoked chicken,
cut in chunks
3–4 hard-boiled eggs, shelled
2 celery hearts, washed
250g/8oz/ blueberries
assorted salad leaves (endive,
chicory, small round lettuce, etc.)
90g/3oz/¼ cup flaked almonds;
toasted
salt and freshly ground black pepper

FOR THE FRENCH
DRESSING
8tbsp extra virgin olive oil
2tbsp white wine vinegar or
blueberry vinegar (see p.75)

FOR THE SOURED
CREAM DRESSING
4tbsp soured cream
3tbsp white wine vinegar or
blueberry vinegar (see p.75)
1tbsp caster (superfine) sugar

If you have bought a whole bird, using a sharp knife, remove all the skin from the chicken, then ease the flesh off the bones – you might find it easier to cut the bird into joints first. Cut the meat in large chunks or pull it into thick strands and reserve.

Separate the yolks from the whites of the eggs. Chop the whites into small dice. Sieve the yolks into a small bowl. Divide the celery into sticks and cut them into small pieces. Reserve a few blueberries for the garnish. Wash and dry the salad leaves.

For the dressings, in separate bowls, mix together all the ingredients for each dressing, adding seasoning to taste.

In a large bowl, using a wooden spoon, mix together the chicken, chopped egg whites, chopped celery and blueberries. Toss lightly with the French dressing, taking care not to bruise the fruit. Check the seasoning.

To serve, make a bed of salad leaves on a large serving plate and arrange the chicken mixture on top of the leaves. Sieve the egg yolks over the salad and season with black pepper. Scatter the toasted almonds and reserved blueberries over the top. Serve the soured cream dressing separately.

Serves 4–6

BLUEBERRY AND PEACH COBBLER

900g/2lb ripe peaches
caster (superfine) sugar, to taste
large pinch each of freshly grated
nutmeg and powdered cinnamon
1tsp lemon juice
450g/1lb blueberries, cleaned
and washed
60g/2oz/¼ cup slivered almonds
crème fraîche or yogurt, to serve

Serves 4–6

FOR THE DOUGH
120g/4oz/1 cup unbleached white flour
1tsp baking powder
1tbsp caster (superfine) sugar
pinch of salt
60g/2oz/4tbsp unsalted butter, cut
in small pieces
1 egg
3tbsp skimmed milk

Preheat the oven to 200°C/400°F/Gas 6.

Peel the peaches and slice them thinly. Put the slices in a saucepan over medium heat and cook them gently until the juice begins to boil. Remove from the heat and allow to cool. Drain off and reserve any excess juice.

Using a wooden spoon, mix together the peaches, sugar (from 4 to 8tbsp, depending on sweetness of the peaches), nutmeg, cinnamon and lemon juice. Set aside.

To make the cobbler dough, sift the flour and baking powder into a large bowl. Stir in the sugar and salt, then rub in the butter until the mixture resembles coarse crumbs.

Using a fork, beat the egg and milk together in a small bowl and add to the flour mixture, mixing all the ingredients together to a dough. Lightly flour your working surface and shape or roll out the dough into a large rectangle about 1cm/½in thick. Cut out six or seven 6.5cm/2½in rounds and reserve.

Pour the peaches into a lightly greased ovenproof dish measuring 18 × 27cm/7 × 9in. Add the blueberries and mix gently. Top with the pastry rounds. Brush with milk, sprinkle with almonds and sugar and bake for 25 minutes. Serve with crème fraîche or yogurt and the peach juices.

ELDERBERRY, BLUEBERRY AND BLACKBERRY JAM

675g/1½lb elderberries
225g/8oz blueberries
900g/2lb blackberries
1.8kg/4lb sugar with pectin
juice of 2 lemons

When using juicy fruit like blackberries it is unnecessary to add water. Put the blackberries in a preserving pan. Using a fork, strip the elderberries from their stalks and add to the blackberries. Add the blueberries. Stir in the sugar and lemon juice.

Bring slowly to the boil stirring often. Boil rapidly for 5–7 minutes, skimming off any scum and seeds that rise to the top. Remove from the heat and test for setting point (see p.26).

When it is ready, spoon into sterilized jars and seal with wax-paper disc and cellophane or screw-top lids.

Makes 3½kg/7½lb

CAPE GOOSEBERRY OR PHYSALIS

This small, golden berry is encased in a veined pod or husk and looks like an
exotic decoration – Chinese lantern is another name for the prettiest
of all berries. This is a luxury berry to be served as an after-dinner treat.
Eat them raw or dip in fondant icing or chocolate. Do not eat the
delicate husks which are thought to be poisonous (after all, it is a member of
the nightshade family). As their name suggests, Cape gooseberries
taste like soft, ripe gooseberries and also have a mild scent. Cape
gooseberries make wonderful – though expensive – jams and cakes.

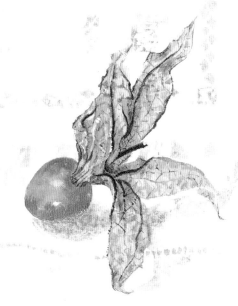

BLACKBERRIES

Blackberries grow throughout the world but are most plentiful in the north. There is evidence that this most prolific of all fruits was eaten in Britain in Neolithic times and, as befits its age, is surrounded by superstitions. In Cornwall, in south-west England, the first blackberry spotted growing each year is thought to banish warts. Many people still believe that you shouldn't eat blackberries after 10 October because 'during the night the Devil goes by and spits on every bush'.

The wild blackberry grows in woodlands and hedgerows and has a sweet yet tart flavour with a lot of seed to flesh. Cultivated blackberries taste nearly as good but are invariably more fleshy and juicy. No fruit is less trouble to grow. Blackberries bruise easily so handle and wash them as little as possible. Ripe berries will keep for only a day or two once picked.

Blackberry sorbets and ice creams are spectacularly purple as are blackberries folded into natural yogurt. Add firm and ripe berries to salads and try serving a blackberry sauce with veal chops.

If you dye your own clothes remember that blackberries were once collected and sold by country folk to create navy blue and indigo.

WILD MUSHROOM SALAD WITH BLACKBERRY VINEGAR

This is one of Frances Bissell's recipes. It can be made with cultivated mushrooms if
you don't have access to wild ones, though the flavours of ceps or
chanterelles take a lot of beating.

450g/1lb mushrooms, cleaned
1 medium red onion or other mild
onion, peeled
salt and freshly ground black pepper
3tbsp walnut oil
3tbsp blackberry vinegar
chopped parsley to garnish
brown bread and butter, to serve

Slice the mushrooms and onions very thinly
and mix them together gently on a white
serving dish. Season.

Heat the oil and vinegar together in a small
saucepan almost to boiling point and pour
over the mushrooms. Leave to cool.

Garnish with the parsley and serve with
bread and butter.

Serves 4

BLACKBERRY VINEGAR

Fruit vinegars make a delicious alternative to wine vinegar in salad dressings, and they also make a useful substitute for wine or other alcohol when deglazing a frying pan (griddle) or roasting pan to make a savoury sauce or gravy. Any type of berry can be used in place of the blackberries. This vinegar takes 3 days to make, so use freshly picked berries for each stage.

1.6kg/3¹/₂lb blackberries
1 litre/32fl oz/1 quart white wine vinegar

Put 450g/1lb of the fruit into a bowl with the vinegar. Cover and allow to stand for at least 24 hours.

Place another 450g/1lb of berries in a separate bowl and strain the liquid from the first batch on to the new fruit. Leave for a further 24 hours, and then repeat the process with another 450g/1lb berries.

Put the remaining 250g/¹/₂lb berries in a clean bottle and strain the vinegar on to the berries. Close tightly with a screw top or cork and set aside to mature for no less than a month.

Makes about 1 litre/32fl oz/1 quart

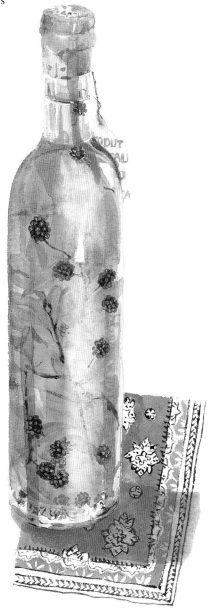

BLACKBERRY MUFFINS

vegetable oil
250g/8oz/2 cups plain (all-purpose) flour
120g/4oz/1/2 cup caster (superfine) sugar
1tsp baking powder
1/2tsp powdered cinnamon
1/2tsp salt
1 egg
90g/3oz blackberries
250ml/8fl oz/1 cup milk

Preheat the oven to 200°C/400°F/Gas 6.
Using a pastry brush, lightly oil twelve
6.5cm/2½in muffin pan cups.

In a large bowl mix together the flour,
sugar, baking powder, cinnamon and salt.

In another bowl, lightly beat the egg with a
fork then stir in the blackberries and add the
milk and 60ml/2fl oz/¼ cup oil. Pour this
mixture straight into the flour and stir just
until the flour has become moistened. Don't
beat the mixture: the batter should be lumpy.

Spoon the batter into the greased muffin
pans and wipe off any spilled batter. Bake in
the preheated oven for about 20–25 minutes
or until the muffins have risen well and a
skewer comes out clean. Remove the muffins
on to a wire rack and serve warm with butter.

Makes 12

BLACKBERRY AND APPLE PIE

FOR THE PASTRY
*250g/8oz/2 cups plain
(all-purpose) flour
½tsp salt
120g/4oz/½ cup chilled
butter, diced
2–3tbsp well-chilled water*

FOR THE FILLING
*900g/2lb cooking apples
1tbsp fresh lemon juice
175g/6oz/¾ cup caster
(superfine) sugar
450g/1lb blackberries*

For the pastry, mix together the flour and salt in a medium bowl and cut in the butter until the mixture resembles breadcrumbs. Sprinkle in the water a little at a time and mix together lightly with a fork until the pastry just holds together. Shape the mixture into a ball, then wrap it in waxed paper and chill for about half an hour.

Preheat the oven to 200°C/400°F/Gas 6.

Core, peel and slice the apples into a lightly greased pie dish, scattering the layers with blackberries and sugar. Heap the fruit into a mound above the rim of the dish.

Roll out the pastry into a circle about 3mm/⅛in thick and about 5cm/2in wider all round than the dish. Fit a narrow strip of pastry round the rim of the dish and dampen with cold water. Place the pastry lid over the dish, seal and trim the edges and cut a ventilation hole in the middle. Bake for 45–60 minutes, reducing the heat slightly when the pastry is lightly coloured. When cooked, sprinkle immediately with sugar and serve.

Serves 6

BRAMBLE CHUTNEY

This is a delicious, spicy-tasting chutney. Slightly runny in consistency, even when set, it goes well with cold meats such as chicken, ham, pork or lamb and makes an ideal accompaniment for roast game. It most definitely improves with age.

1kg/2lb cooking apples
3kg/6lb blackberries
1kg/2lb onions
1kg/2lb soft brown sugar
1.25 litres/2 pints/5 cups vinegar
30ml/2tbsp salt
50g/2oz mustard powder
50g/2oz ground ginger or
2.5cm/1in stick fresh ginger
root, trimmed
10ml/2tsp ground nutmeg or mace
5ml/1tsp cayenne pepper

Peel, core and chop the apples. Wash the blackberries. Skin and chop the onions. Put the fruit into a large preserving pan or kettle and add all the remaining ingredients.

Bring to the boil and then reduce the heat and, stirring constantly with a wooden spoon, simmer uncovered for 2–2½ hours or until the mixture thickens.

Spoon or pour into clean, hot jars or preserving glasses. Cover with discs of waxed paper and seal when cold.

Makes about 4kg/8lb

CRANBERRIES

Thanksgiving and Christmas would not be the same without cranberries, the name given by the early settlers in America to these rich, ruby-red berries, because the flower stamens form a 'beak' resembling that of a crane.

The United States is the largest producer of cranberries, although a smaller version grows in boggy parts of the north of England and in Scotland. The Scandinavian lingonberry is of the same family and can be used instead of cranberries in most recipes.

Cranberries are rarely eaten raw and it is surprising that the North American Indians who introduced early Pilgrims to the berry persevered long enough to discover ways of making a virtue of their taste, which is more sour and bitter than any other fruit.

Having said this, the boldness of cranberries is a godsend in creating distinctive sauces, soups, breads, tarts, pâtés, relishes, salsas, ice

creams and sorbets, as the jewel-rich colour and sharp flavour contrast strongly with the other ingredients.

Cranberry soup is particularly delicious and a perfect first course for clearing the palate when a rich dish is to follow. Serve cranberry sauce with turkey, cold if you must but hot is better with the addition of spice, alcohol or mint leaves. If you are grilling a fish that needs livening up, serve cranberry sauce to the side. It is easy to make your own sauce, but never cook the berries with sugar since this toughens the skin. Add the sugar when the skins have popped. Serve a rich meaty gravy, which contains a few lightly cooked berries, with roast duck, lamb and chicken.

Next Christmas, as well as cooking these berries, decorate your fir tree with aromatic and colourful threads of cranberries, popcorn and cinnamon sticks.

CRANBERRY SOUP

This is a delicious and very colourful soup for serving hot in the festive season when
the berries are in plentiful supply. Garnish it with fronds of fresh
fennel, reflecting the colours of Christmas.

30g/1oz/2tbsp butter
1tbsp cooking oil
*1 medium onion, peeled and
finely chopped*
3 sticks celery, washed and trimmed
2 medium carrots, peeled
2 cloves garlic, peeled and chopped
*300ml/10fl oz/1¼ cups fresh
orange juice*
*700g/1½lb tomatoes, skinned,
deseeded and chopped or 2 × 400g/
2 × 14oz cans of tomatoes*
2tbsp caster (superfine) sugar
salt and pepper to taste
2 whole cloves
pinch of mace
1 bay leaf
½ stick cinnamon
250g/8oz fresh or frozen cranberries
fronds of fresh fennel, to garnish

Heat the butter and oil together in a large pan
over low heat. Add the finely chopped onion
and cook gently for about 5 minutes or until
transparent. Add the chopped celery and
carrot and cook together gently with the
onion for 2 minutes.

Add all the remaining ingredients except the
cranberries and fennel, along with 625ml/
20fl oz/2½ cups water. Cover and bring to
the boil, then reduce the heat and simmer for
30 minutes.

Chop up 175g/6oz of the cranberries, add to
the soup and simmer for 10 minutes. If you
are using fresh cranberries, cook the
remaining berries in boiling water for 8
minutes and reserve them for the garnish.

To serve, remove and discard the whole
spices. Adjust the seasoning if you wish.
Pour the soup into individual serving
bowls. Garnish with a frond of fennel and
some of the whole cranberries.

Serves 6

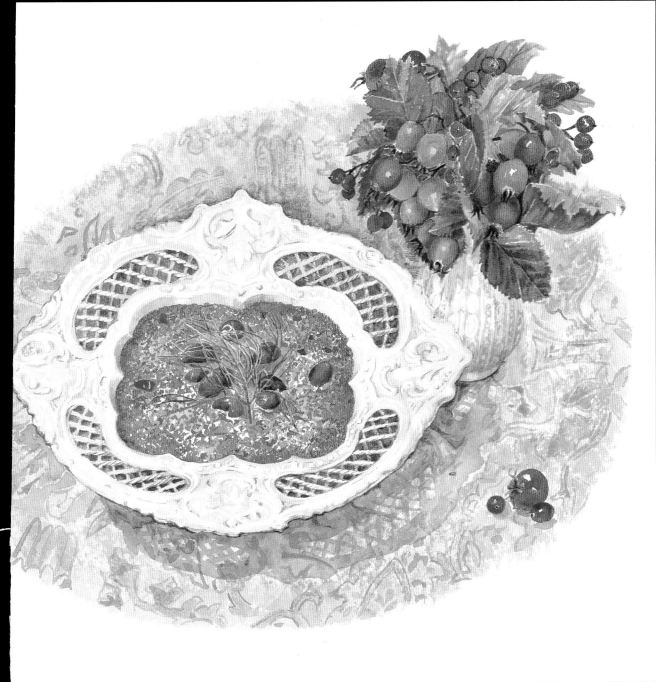

CRANBERRY NUT BREAD

*250g/8oz/2 cups plain (all-purpose)
flour, plus a little extra for the fruit
90g/3oz/⅓ cup caster
(superfine) sugar
2tsp baking powder
½tsp salt
1½tsp mixed spice
1 medium egg, beaten
175ml/6fl oz/¾ cup milk
2tbsp melted butter
175g/6oz fresh or frozen cranberries
60g/2oz/⅓ cup coarsely chopped
walnuts or pecans
30g/1oz/2tbsp raisins or sultanas
(golden raisins)
finely grated zest (rind) of 1 orange*

Preheat the oven to 180°C/350°F/Gas 4, and lightly grease a 20×11.5×7.5cm/8×4½×3in loaf tin. Sift the flour, sugar, baking powder, salt and mixed spice into a large bowl. Make a well in the centre and pour in the egg, milk and butter. Mix together well with a wooden spoon.

In a separate bowl, toss the cranberries, nuts, raisins and orange zest in the extra flour, then fold this into the batter.

Pour the mixture into the prepared loaf tin and bake in the preheated oven for 45–50 minutes or until the bread pulls away from the sides of the tin and a skewer inserted in the centre comes out clean.

Remove from the oven and leave to cool in the tin for about 10 minutes before turning out to finish cooling on a wire rack. Wrap in foil and keep for 24 hours before serving.

Makes one 450g/1lb loaf

CRANBERRY RELISH

This traditional recipe from America has been passed on to me by Glynn Christian.
If refrigerated, it will keep for at least a month.

2 small lemons
2 large oranges
1 large cooking apple

450g/1lb fresh or frozen cranberries
250g/8oz/1 cup sugar, or to taste
6tbsp brandy or vodka

Wash the citrus fruits well, cut them in quarters and remove all the pips. Cut the apple into quarters. Roughly chop the citrus fruits in a blender or food processor. Add the apple and chop roughly. Add the cranberries and process just until the berries are cut up. Turn all the chopped fruit into a large bowl and add the sugar and alcohol. Cover and leave at room temperature for 24 hours.

Taste the relish and add more sugar if you wish. The fruit will have begun to soften and the flavours to blend. Spoon out into clean, dry, airtight jars and store for at least a week before serving.

Makes about 900g/2lb

AVRIL

⅖ Campari
⅕ blackberry liqueur
(liqueur de mûres)
⅖ tonic water

Mix all the ingredients together in the quantities required in the above proportions. Avril is usually served in tall martini glasses.

FRUIT CUP

2.3 litres/4 pints/2½ quarts white
wine, chilled
250ml/8fl oz/1 cup crème de cassis
1 litre/1¾ pints/1 quart tropical
fruit juice, chilled
600ml/1 pint/2½ cups sparkling
mineral water, chilled

TO DECORATE
Sprigs of fresh mint, raspberries,
strawberries, blueberries

Mix the *crème de cassis*, white wine and fruit juice together in a large glass jug (pitcher) and chill.

When ready to serve, pour in the mineral water and decorate with sprigs of mint and fresh berries.

INDEX OF RECIPE TITLES